GEOGRAPHY ENCYCLOPEDIA

ATMOSPHERE

Om Books International

CONTENTS

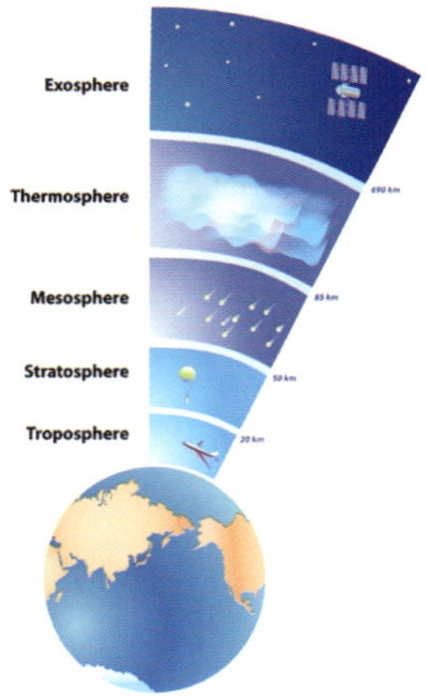
Exosphere
Thermosphere
Mesosphere
Stratosphere
Troposphere

EARTH'S ATMOSPHERE

Our spherical Earth is encircled by the invisible atmosphere. This atmosphere also encircles all other planets. The atmosphere is composed of several gases that exist in varying quantities in different layers. Though the atmosphere is composed of gases, it has weight. The bottommost layer of the atmosphere accounts for most of its mass.

Earth's atmosphere has undergone many changes since the time of its formation. The first atmosphere was considered to be "reducing atmosphere" as, according to most scientists, it contained little or no oxygen. Today, about 99 per cent of the atmosphere is oxygen and nitrogen. So, today's atmosphere is called "oxidising atmosphere".

WHAT IS ATMOSPHERE?

Atmosphere is more often than not described as a blanket of air surrounding Earth. The air is made up of several gases such as nitrogen, oxygen, argon, carbon dioxide, helium and neon. There are some other gases that are present in very small percentages. The atmosphere also has dry air and water vapour.

Life without atmosphere

All planets have atmospheres. But, the atmosphere of each planet is very different. Some celestial bodies do not have an atmosphere. If Earth did not have an atmosphere, we would not exist. This is because Earth's atmosphere contains oxygen. This oxygen is present in the air we breathe. The atmosphere protects Earth from harmful radiations emerging from the Sun. It also keeps the heat in check. Besides this, it also makes sure that the Sun's heat does not escape into space. The atmosphere is also a necessary factor behind the water cycle.

Sunrays piercing through the atmosphere.

Layers of the atmosphere

Scientists have studied the structure of the atmosphere and defined six layers in its structure. These layers are the troposphere, the stratosphere, the mesosphere, the ionosphere, the thermosphere and the exosphere, where the troposphere is the closest to Earth's surface. There is no clear boundary or line dividing these structures. These divisions are made on the basis of the temperature in each of the layers.

An illustration of the layers of the atmosphere.

FUN FACT

The atmosphere extends to more than 500 km from Earth's surface. There is no clear division between outer space and Earth's atmosphere; however, the closer we go to outer space, the less the cover of gases.

Early atmosphere

Not much is definitively known of the early atmosphere. What is known for sure is that the atmosphere has seen many changes over a period of millions of years.

As time passed, the original atmosphere was slowly lost while compounds let out from young Earth's crust permeated the air. As comets and asteroids crashed into Earth, their matter created a change in the atmosphere.

EARLY ATMOSPHERE

It is believed that Earth's current atmosphere contains less carbon dioxide and greater quantities of nitrogen and oxygen than it did in the past. It is also believed that there was a time, billions of years ago, when Earth did not have an atmosphere at all. The gradual changes in the atmosphere are what led to the birth of life on Earth.

The first atmosphere

Billions of years ago, when Earth was formed, it had many volcanoes on the surface. These volcanoes let out gases and constantly underwent volcanic activity. This went on for nearly a billion years. At this time, the atmosphere mainly contained carbon dioxide gas with (presumably) no oxygen. Ammonia, methane and water vapour were also present, they were in much smaller quantities. When Earth cooled, the water vapour in the air is said to have condensed to form the water on Earth's surface.

The eruption of a volcano.

Photosynthetic organisms

"Photosynthetic organisms" is the name given to the earliest organisms on Earth that were able to carry out the process of photosynthesis. There are many theories on these organisms and their effect on Earth's early atmosphere, though most of these theories remain unverified.

After their appearance, oxygen either formed or its amount in the atmosphere increased (if it already existed). During the process of photosynthesis, an organism takes carbon dioxide from the air and gives out oxygen. As a result, the amount of carbon dioxide in the atmosphere began to reduce.

Oxygen in the rocks

A lot of the oxygen first produced by the photosynthetic organisms was absorbed by rocks and the red beds in the continental crust. It is believed that even today the ancient red beds and rocks contain oxygen in them. Nearly one billion years ago, some rocks became saturated by oxygen and began to let out oxygen into the air.

Formation of the ozone layer

The amount of oxygen in the air increased when rocks began to let out oxygen. The frequency of emissions and explosions in volcanoes also reduced. This helped send out more oxygen into the atmosphere and in greater quantities. Sunlight acted upon oxygen to produce the ozone layer. This is when life evolved on the planet.

Beneton Hills, Capital Reef Park, Utah.

THE TURBULENT TROPOSPHERE

Troposphere is the layer which is closest to Earth's surface. The weather processes take place in this layer. It holds clouds in the sky. Due to this, the height of the troposphere varies in different parts of the world. When it is above a water body or towards the poles, it is 8 km from the surface. When it is above the equator, it is 16 km from the surface.

Tropopause

The tropopause is the topmost layer of the troposphere. The area in the troposphere where the temperature drops as low as -56 °C marks the beginning of the tropopause. Just like the height of the troposphere, the height of the tropopause varies at the poles and the equator. The height is greater in the summer than in the winter. This is also true for the troposphere.

Weather in the troposphere

About 90 per cent of the atmosphere's water vapour is contained within the troposphere. This water vapour forms clouds, fog and takes other forms. Wind blows strongly in the troposphere and carries air masses from the high-pressure systems to the low-pressure systems. The weather systems are changed here so that we experience different weather through the course of a day.

Clouds formed in the troposphere.

Meteorological marvels

The meteorological phenomena that we marvel over takes place in the troposphere. These phenomena occur due to radiation from the Sun and the rotation of Earth.

Thinning air

Mountain climbers, especially those wanting to climb to the peak of Mount Everest, have always been advised to carry oxygen cylinders with them. This is because as we go higher into the troposphere, the air thins. The oxygen molecules greatly reduce in number. The top of Mount Everest has fewer oxygen molecules. Which is why, to breathe easier, mountain climbers are asked to carry oxygen cylinders. Mountain tops are also cold and have snow because, as the air thins, the temperature cools drastically.

Meteorologists observe the troposphere to get an idea of the weather.

THE CALM STRATOSPHERE

As most of the weather processes take place in the troposphere, it experiences sudden and drastic changes. However, the layer above it, the stratosphere, is much more stable and peaceful. We can roughly consider the uppermost part of the tropopause as the boundary between the troposphere and the stratosphere. The stratosphere extends from about 14 km to above Earth's surface.

Aeroplanes fly in the lower stratosphere.

What can one see in the stratosphere?

Aeroplanes avoid the turbulence that can be caused while flying in the quickly changing conditions of the troposphere. Though the stratosphere does experience forceful winds, it still remains calm. Air in the stratosphere flows horizontally.

Aeroplanes avoid the turbulence that can be caused while flying in the quickly changing conditions of the troposphere. Though the stratosphere does experience forceful winds, it still remains calm. Air in the stratosphere flows horizontally.

Temperature and thickness

The temperature in the stratosphere increases from the troposphere due to a thin layer of the ozone. It reaches nearly 0 °C. However, as seen in the troposphere, the air pressure continues to reduce as we go higher and higher. Similar to the troposphere, there is a variation to the thickness of the stratosphere based on what it is above. The stratosphere is thicker at the poles and above water bodies but thinner at the equator.

The orange layer is the troposphere, the whitish layer is the stratosphere and the bluish layer is the mesosphere.

The ozone

Perhaps the most important feature of the stratosphere is that it contains ozone. Ozone is a form of oxygen. It blocks the ultraviolet rays of the Sun from reaching Earth's surface. These rays are also called "UV rays" and are considered very harmful to the environment.

Ozone depletion

Ozone lies in a very thin layer in the stratosphere. This layer is called the "ozone layer". The cover of this layer has been steadily declining, which is a topic of much concern for scientists everywhere. It is believed that the use of harmful chemicals such as chlorofluorocarbons (CFCs) has led to the decrease in the cover of the ozone layer. This is called "ozone depletion".

Oxygen levels deplete as you go higher above the sea level.

THE FREEZING MESOSPHERE

The layer above the stratosphere is the mesosphere. Starting at the uppermost boundary of the stratosphere, the mesosphere extends to about 85 km higher. The temperature, which rose to 0 °C at the stratosphere, begins to drop again in the mesosphere.

Information on the mesosphere

Of all layers of the atmosphere, the lowest temperatures are seen at the mesosphere. The uppermost boundary of the mesosphere is called the "mesopause". As the mesosphere is so high up in the atmosphere, a study and research of it is very difficult. Air transport such as aeroplanes and aircraft cannot go here as it is too high up. It would be unsafe to try and explore this layer with such means of transport. Sending a spacecraft to explore this layer is also not possible as it is too low in the atmosphere. In the past, meteorologists and scientists have sent unmanned rockets to find information about this layer. These rockets have collected some data during their journey.

Sprites and elves

Sprites and elves are two things that are said to exist in the mesosphere. Very little is known about them. Sprites are said to be electrical discharges that appear red in colour. They have vertical movement. On the other hand, elves are halo-shaped electrical discharges that are very dim.

Only rockets can survive in the mesosphere.

Noctilucent clouds

The temperature at the mesosphere dips to nearly 0 °C. Due to its extremely low temperatures, the water vapour in the mesosphere freezes to form noctilucent clouds. They are also called "night-shining clouds" or "ice clouds" and are nothing but frozen water. Sometimes, after a sunset, one can see tiny, wispy clouds far away in the sky. These might be the noctilucent clouds.

Noctilucent clouds over Estonia.

Shooting stars

When meteors crash into the atmosphere, the dust and rocks left behind is let out into the mesosphere. These dust and rock particles are visible in the mesosphere and can sometimes be seen on Earth as shooting stars. Some shooting stars are large and carry a lot of heat and pressure. They fall from the mesosphere and sometimes land on Earth's surface.

THE THICK THERMOSPHERE

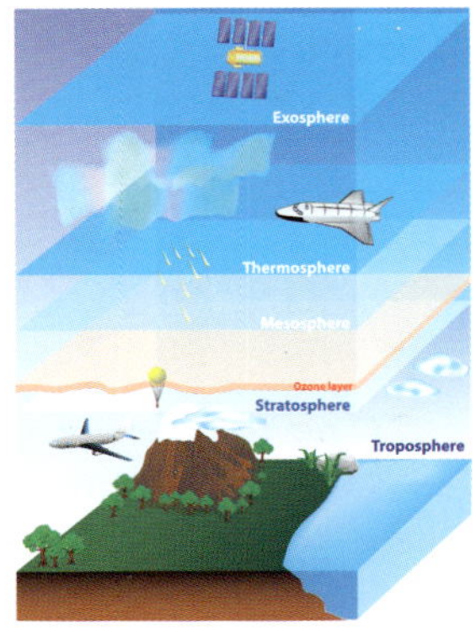

The thermosphere contains the lighter gases of the atmosphere such as oxygen, helium and hydrogen. It starts from the uppermost part of the mesosphere and extends to a distance of 690 km from Earth's surface.

Thermosphere

Like the ozone layer, some UV rays are absorbed in the thermosphere. It is said to be the thickest of all layers. We know more about this layer than the mesosphere because the Hubble Space Telescope and the International Space Station make their orbits around Earth in this layer.

The Hubble Space Telescope helped us learn more about this layer.

Action on electrons

There are solar protons present in the thermosphere which act upon the electrons here. These solar protons contain high levels of energy. They tear away electrons from the gas molecules and particles present in this layer. This creates an electric charge in the layer for the ions of the atoms and molecules present here. Even the ionosphere contains these ions.

The ions and protons that are charged in the thermosphere clash with the atoms and molecules present here. These atoms get rid of the extra energy by giving out light. The colourful aurora we see on Earth is nothing but this light.

Aurora borealis is also called the "Northern Lights".

Lack of heat transfer

The molecules of gases present in this layer absorb the UV rays and x-rays present here. This causes the molecules to move at great speed and create high temperatures. The temperatures at the thermosphere rise to nearly 1500 °C. However, there is no heat in this layer. This is because the molecules do not transfer energy from one to the other. There is very little pressure in this area which does not allow for the transfer of energy or heat.

This layer is known for absorbing UV rays.

Differing temperatures of day and night

It is believed that the temperature at the thermosphere is hotter during the day than at night. This is because of the solar energy received from the Sun. The temperatures during the daytime tend to rise to 200 °C. If the Sun is active, the temperature rises to 500 °C from 200 °C.

THE FLUCTUATING EXOSPHERE

The exosphere is the outermost layer of the atmosphere. It lies about 500 km above Earth's surface. The area between the exosphere and the thermosphere, which fluctuates in temperature and pressure, is called "turbopause". The lowermost part of the exosphere, which lies right above the turbopause, is called "exobase".

Expanding and contracting

The exosphere frequently comes into contact with solar storms. It expands and contracts as and when a solar storm occurs in or around it. Explosive activities on the solar surface cause particles to be flung into the outer space. Due to these solar storms, the exosphere's distance from Earth's surface could increase to about 1000 km. As the Sun becomes calmer, the distance could increase to 10,000 km.

Geocorona taken by NASA.

Geocorona

The geocorona is a vague blue light that circles Earth. This is formed from the neutral hydrogen atoms present in the exosphere. The geocorona is a solar, ultraviolet light that is reflected from the hydrogen atoms of the exosphere. It is visible in the satellite photos of Earth. It is estimated to be about 1,00,000 km from Earth's surface.

Solar activity

Solar storms can be caused for various reasons. An eruption of energy and mass or such activity which takes place on the surface of the Sun is called a "solar storm". These activities can either be solar flares, solar wind which moves in great speed, release of solar particles containing high energy, or coronal mass ejections. These activities take place because of the magnetic field of the Sun.

Gases present in the exosphere

The exosphere mainly contains hydrogen. Hydrogen is the lightest of all gases. As a result, the atmosphere at the exosphere is very thin. The exosphere also contains helium, oxygen and carbon dioxide.

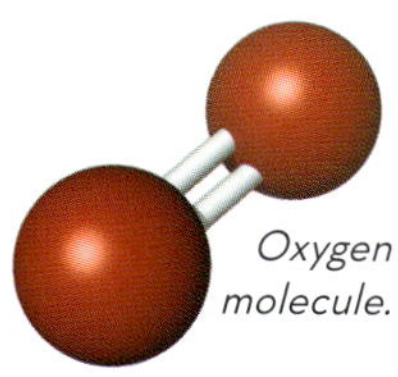

Oxygen molecule.

Carbon dioxide molecule.

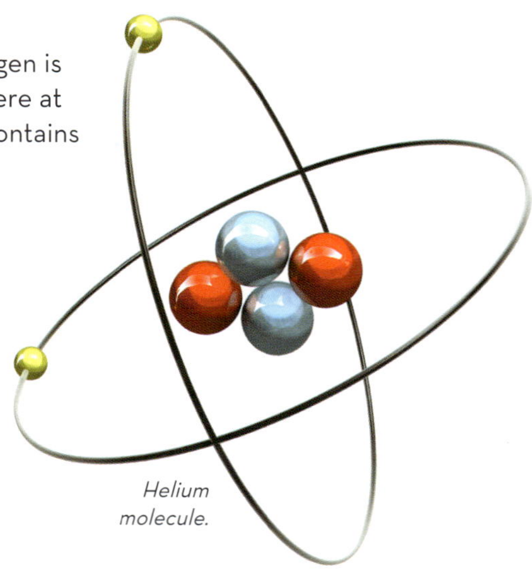

Helium molecule.

THE ENERGETIC IONOSPHERE

The ionosphere is named after the ions that are present here. These ions are created from particles of sunlight. They contain a lot of energy.

Layers of the ionosphere

When atoms come into contact with x-rays, some of the electrons get separated from them. This creates ions and free electrons. They are called "D", "E", "F1" and "F2". As observed in all layers of the atmosphere, the extent of the four layers of the ionosphere is different during day and night, and the different seasons.

What are ions?

An ion is charged atom where the number of protons and electrons are unequal. If an ion has more electrons than protons, it gives out a negative charge. If it has more protons than electrons, it gives out a positive charge.

Path of the radio waves

The ions and free electrons present in the ionosphere reflect radio waves. In 1901, Guglielmo Marconi sent out a radio signal from England, from a place called Cornwall. This signal was sent to a place called Newfoundland in Canada.

The intention behind this experiment was to find proof of the theory that the path taken by radio waves depended upon the atmosphere. It was incorrectly believed that radio waves travelled on a straight path. This experiment proved that radio waves travelled by bouncing off the ions in the ionosphere.

Guglielmo Marconi.

Disappearing layers of the ionosphere

The D and E layers of the ionosphere are the layers that are closest to Earth. During the night, these layers disappear. As a result of this disappearance, radio waves are undisturbed by the ions and, therefore, are able to travel higher into the air. This is why, at night, radio stations are able to extend their reach by more than a hundred kilometres.

The undisturbed radio wave phenomenon is especially true for AM radio. AM radio, or amplitude modification, is a method of communicating by radio. This communication takes place by sending signals that vary in strength.

A telecommunications station.

ATMOSPHERES OF OTHER PLANETS

Like Earth, all the other seven planets in the solar system have their own atmospheres. Each planet's atmosphere is different from the other. However, they do have some similarities.

Atmospheres of terrestrial planets

Mercury, Venus, Earth and Mars are terrestrial planets. Their atmospheres are quite similar to each other. Most of the layers are also the same. Here are some special features of the atmospheres of terrestrial planets:

- **Mercury**
  It has a thin exosphere. Its exosphere is mainly occupied by a lot of hydrogen atoms. Helium and oxygen atoms are also present here.

- **Venus**
  It is considered to be Earth's twin. But it has a thicker atmosphere than Earth. This is why we cannot see the planet clearly from Earth. Its layers contain clouds of sulphuric acid. The major gas present here is carbon dioxide.

- **Mars**
  Carbon dioxide is also largely present in Mars's atmosphere. However, its atmosphere is much thinner than Venus's atmosphere.

Atmospheres of gas giants

Jupiter, Saturn, Uranus and Neptune are popularly known as "gas giants". The atmospheres of these planets are composed of, as well as dominated by, a multitude of gases. The atmospheres of all gas giants have helium and hydrogen gases in large quantities.

Jupiter's atmosphere

The lower layers of Jupiter's atmosphere have ammonia and hydrogen sulphide clouds, which form bands around the planet. These clouds form light or dark-coloured bands. The light-coloured ones are called "zones" while the dark-coloured ones are called "belts". As Jupiter spins quickly, it creates fast wind. This fast wind clearly separates the different coloured bands.

Saturn's atmosphere

Like Jupiter, Saturn's atmosphere also has bands of light and dark colours. These bands are sometimes struck by lightning or cyclones. This forms patterns on the bands. Even Jupiter is affected by such natural occurrences.

Titan, Saturn's moon, has its own atmosphere made up of nitrogen and methane. The moon appears to be orange due to the effect of methane on the sunlight received by Titan.

The solar system.

EARTH'S ENERGY BUDGET

The Sun gives out light, heat and energy. These are absorbed by the atmosphere and then spread to Earth. There are different ways of absorbing these gifts from the Sun. "Earth's budget" is the amount of light, heat and energy it takes from the Sun.

Radiative equilibrium

Heat from the atmosphere is moved to Earth. Then, by wind and water, this heat is moved to different parts of Earth. Heat is also sent to the surface and lower atmosphere. From here it is sent back to outer space. Earth's temperature remains stable from a long period of time when the amount of heat that is taken from and sent back to the atmosphere is the same. This balanced give and take of heat is called "radiative equilibrium".

Solar energy

The energy from the Sun that reaches Earth's atmosphere is absorbed by different sources. Nearly 29 per cent of the total energy given out by the Sun is returned or reflected back to outer space by clouds. Other particles of the atmosphere, ice, snow and sea also reflect this energy back to outer space.

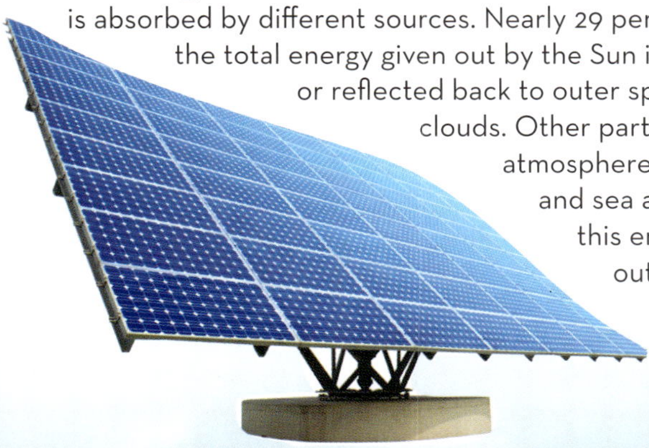

Absorption of solar energy

Nearly 23 per cent of the solar energy sent to Earth is absorbed by the ozone, the dust and the water vapour in the upper and lower layers of the atmosphere. Less than 50 per cent of the solar energy reaches Earth's surface. This energy is then absorbed by the surface. This shows that a little more than 70 per cent of the total solar energy sent to Earth is absorbed by the different parts of it. Heat escapes from such areas that have warm climates and very few clouds. If an area has lots of clouds, less heat can escape it.

Sunlight

Sunlight absorbed by the atmosphere and Earth's surface is kept controlled and balanced by the heat from the atmosphere and the surface. About 71 per cent of solar radiation is absorbed by the atmosphere.

HOT AND COLD

The most important factor behind the world's climate is the temperature. Earth and its atmosphere receive heat from the Sun. It is the primary source of heat. Heat is also received from other celestial bodies and from Earth's interior. However, without the Sun, Earth and its atmosphere would not receive enough heat.

Factors affecting the temperature

There are certain factors determining the temperature of a particular place on Earth's surface.

- **Latitudes:**
  Latitudes play an important role in controlling temperature. The temperature of an area on Earth is largely determined by the way the Sun's rays strike Earth. The Sun's rays hit different parts of Earth at different angles. This is because of the tilt of Earth's axis which is tilted at 23.4°.

  Generally, the temperature is highest at the equator where the Sun's rays hit Earth directly and horizontally. Temperature is lowest at the North Pole and the South Pole because there are few slanting rays. The Poles, as a result, tend to be cooler.

- **Elevation:**
  On Earth, the temperature is lower at places that are at higher elevations or altitudes. This means that the temperature decreases with an increase in the height on the surface. This is why the peaks of tall mountains are cold and covered in snow. Their temperature is much cooler than the temperature at plains.

- **Differences in heating and cooling:**
  Land and water do not cope with heat in the same way, nor do they react to heat in the same way. A piece of land is heated and cooled much quicker than a strip of water. Even if the two received the same amount of sunlight, this variation would still exist. Also, the surface of a water body might feel warm, but if you dip into the water and go deeper, you would realise that the inside is not heated.

- **Ocean currents:**
  Ocean currents play an important role in controlling the temperature on Earth's surface. Usually, ocean currents move from areas with warm temperatures to areas with cooler temperatures. They spread heat to the cooler areas and then bring some of this cool air back to the warmer parts, and vice versa. For example, cold ocean currents move from the Polar Regions to the equator and the warm currents from the equator move to the Poles. Therefore, the coastal regions near the equator are warmer and experience hotter climate than the coasts of the Polar Regions.

The warm and cool ocean currents mingle to create waves.

- **Cloudiness:**
  "Cloudiness" is another factor that affects the temperature of any surface on Earth. It also affects Earth's atmosphere. Cloudiness basically means how many clouds are present in the sky. An area of the sky with too many clouds has a different effect on temperature than a place which has very few clouds.

  With more clouds, the sunrays received by Earth reduces while, with fewer clouds, it increases. The number of sunrays is less because of the presence of the thick cloud cover and hence, the daytime temperature is also reduced.

FUN FACT

Heat is transmitted artificially with the use of certain metals such as copper. These metals are said to be good conductors of heat.

Radiation and conduction

Heat is transmitted by the processes of radiation, conduction and convection. Radiation is the process of transmission of heat. This happens in the form of electromagnetic waves. Conduction is a process where heat is transferred through collisions between neighbouring molecules. Radiation is the transfer of energy through electromagnetic waves. This form of energy does not require the presence of matter and can travel through empty space. It is through this process that most of the Sun's energy is transferred through space from the Sun to Earth.

A magnifying glass can channel heat to one fixed spot.

Altocumulus clouds indicate that the process of convection is taking place in the troposphere.

Convection

Convection is a process of heat transfer by movement of a fluid such as air and water.

The air above a warm place is heated. When this happens, the air expands. This makes it lighter and causes it to rise upwards. As it does this, the cooler air takes its original place. The rising warm air slowly cools as it goes further up and becomes heavier. These currents of cool and warm air are called convection currents.

STATIC STRUCTURE

The density and mass of the atmosphere is a tricky topic. While making any calculations about Earth's atmosphere, its temperature, density and pressure are taken into consideration. Together, they are called the "static structure" of the atmosphere.

Temperature variation

The troposphere is the layer of atmosphere which has the maximum mass of air and the maximum temperature. The temperature is maximum here because it is the closest to Earth's surface. Air receives heat from underground activities and from the surface.

If the sky is not very cloudy, then the air near the surface receives the maximum heat from sunrays. As we go higher up into the air, the temperature lowers because it receives less heat from the surface and there are more clouds present here.

Temperatures vary according to the geography of a region.

Number density

The number of air molecules per unit volume is called a "number density". It is used to calculate the density of air. The air molecules present in the atmospheric layers around Earth are held by gravity. This gives air weight. Air's weight squeezes its molecules together, compressing it so that the number density increases.

If there is more air above a part of Earth's surface, it has more weight and a greater number density.

Temperature inversions

There are thin parts of the atmosphere which get warmer with higher altitude. This is called "temperature inversions". Meteorologists keep an eye on these layers while forecasting the weather. During the winter months, air near the surface might experience temperature inversions. If the inversion is strong, it means there is a difference between the cool surface air and the warmer air.

The air above Earth's surface has the highest number density.

Hydrostatic balance

The pressure in the atmosphere is dependent upon the number density of air. If the atmosphere were static, then the pressure by air exerted in each of the layers would be completely dependent upon number density. The balance between pressure and density is called "hydrostatic balance". A common feature between pressure and density is that they are closely related to height.

THE PUSH AND PULL OF AIR

Air has weight and this weight allows air to push and press against everything around it. This is called "pressure" or "air pressure". In terms of the air in the atmosphere, it is called "atmospheric pressure". Atmospheric pressure is the force that air exerts upon Earth's surface as it is being pushed down upon by gravity.

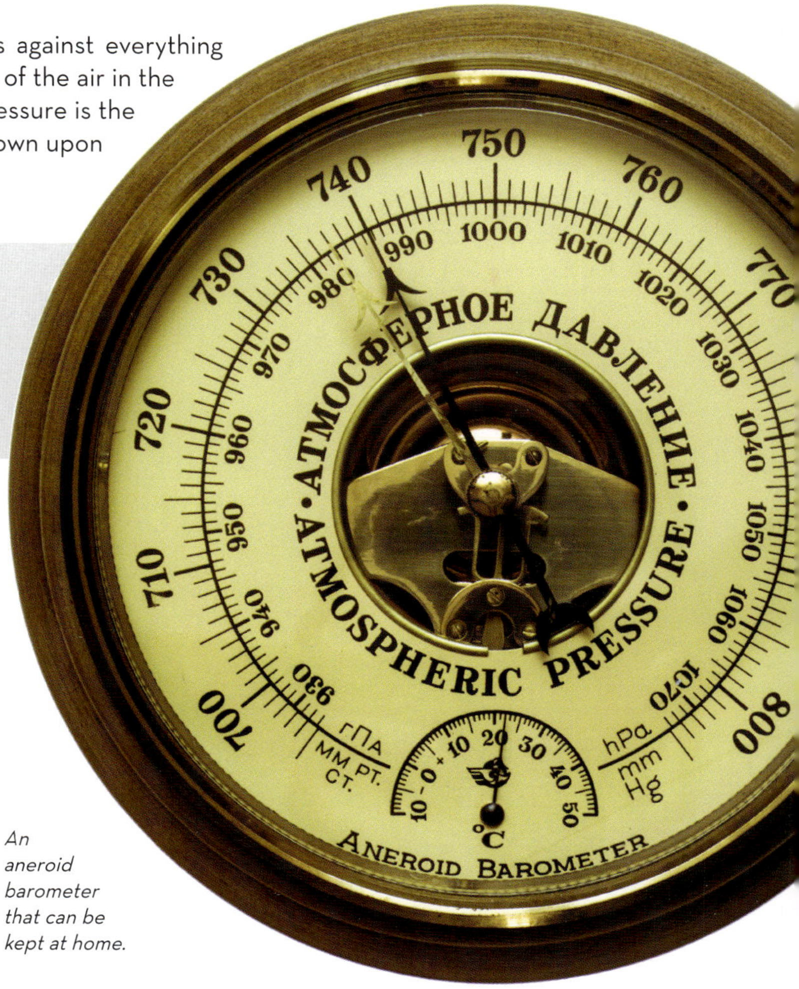

An aneroid barometer that can be kept at home.

Barometer

A device called "barometer" is used to measure atmospheric pressure. This device has a glass tube with liquid mercury. As the weight of the air in the atmosphere increases or decreases, the mercury in the barometer rises or falls. The rising mercury helps determine the weight of the atmosphere.

Unit of atmospheric pressure

Atmospheric pressure is expressed in a unit called "millimetre". An atmosphere (whose unit is "atm") is the average air pressure at sea level at a given temperature of 15 °C. One atmosphere is equal to 760 mm of mercury. Atmospheric pressure is measured in comparison to this unit.

Oxygen and atmospheric pressure

The oxygen in the air decreases with a decrease in the atmospheric pressure. At great elevations and altitudes, the atmospheric pressure is low. This is another reason that the amount of oxygen in the air is also low.

Oxygen cylinders

Mountaineers carry oxygen cylinders while climbing because the air at high altitudes is thinner. Thinner air decreases the oxygen available for breathing and can lead to a condition called "hypoxia".

Oxygen cylinder.

Artificial pressure

The interiors of aircraft and aeroplanes have artificial air pressure so that the people within have enough oxygen and feel comfortable.

Atmospheric pressure and weather

There are two atmospheric pressure systems. These are "low-pressure system" and "high-pressure system". These systems determine the weather and weather patterns of any place. A place that has high-pressure systems will experience stable and calm weather. A place that has low-pressure systems will experience cloudy and windy weather with more precipitation.

THE MOVING BORDERS

Wind is what dries clothes and shakes the leaves of a tree. Strong winds can ruin your hairstyle while light winds can make you feel cool during a hot day. Not all parts of Earth receive the same amount of heat. Heat is spread very unevenly around Earth. Air moves according to the heat received by different parts of Earth. This moving air is called "wind". The wind has certain patterns.

Movement of wind

Atmospheric pressure is received in different amounts in different areas. Wind is generated by these differences in atmospheric pressure. Wind begins to blow at areas with high-pressure systems and then moves to areas with low-pressure systems. These areas have a clear boundary called "front".

Approaching weather fronts can be seen from the land.

Weather front

A front can be in a vertical or horizontal direction. The area within which a front extends is called "frontal zone". It is affected by which air masses or pressure systems it lies between. Air masses, their fronts and the effect they have on each other cause different weather and weather patterns. There are five types of fronts:

- **Stationary front:**
  As the name suggests, this front does not move. It is originally another front which then stops moving. After some time, it begins to move forward and changes into, or resumes being another type of front. A person passing by a stationary front will surely experience a change in the temperature and direction of the wind.
- **Cold front:**
  This front lies between a cold air mass and a warm air mass. This front moves from a northwest direction and goes towards the southeast direction. While moving from this front, a person might notice that the wind and temperature were first warmer and then gradually became cooler. As a cold front moves forward, the temperatures drop to nearly 15°C.

Stationary fronts remain still and might remain over an area for a very long time. If there is a lot of water vapour in the warmer air mass, it might cause heavy or freezing rain.

- **Warm front:**
  This front lies between a warm air mass and a cold air mass. It moves from the southeast towards the northeast. It leaves behind moist and warm air. As it passes through an area, the air becomes warmer and the humidity in the air increases.

Ahead of the warm front, one can see the stratus clouds.

- **Occluded front:**
  An occluded front is formed when a cold front overtakes a warm front. The warm front has cooler air towards the north. An occluded front can easily turn into a cyclone. The cyclone can then move towards the north of the warm front. Once the intensity of the storm increases, the cold front begins to rotate faster and catches up to the warm front. The occluded front is then formed and it separates the cooler air mass from the cold air mass to the north of the warm front.

Prevailing winds

"Prevailing" means "dominant" or "important". A prevailing wind moves in one particular direction over a particular point on the surface of Earth.

Barring a few, most prevailing winds move in the east-west direction. This occurs because of Earth's rotation. Some might even move in the north-south direction. However, this is a rare occurrence. Two prevailing winds from different directions might sometimes meet each other on their path. The area where this meeting occurs is called a "convergence zone".

Prevailing winds are affected by the Coriolis effect. This causes winds to turn in a clockwise direction in the Southern Hemisphere and an anti-clockwise direction in the Northern Hemisphere.

Tropical cyclones sometimes precede the occluded front as it is created when a cold front overtakes a warm front.

Geostrophic winds

Due to the Coriolis effect, some winds move along the edges of the high-pressure and low-pressure systems. These are called "geostrophic winds". These winds are balanced by a combination of the Coriolis effect and Pressure Gradient forces.

When the wind is relatively stationary, it moves from a high pressure area to a low pressure area due the pressure gradient force. However, as this wind moves from a high pressure area to a low pressure area, it is impacted by the Coriolis effect, which causes it to be displaced. This displacement increases as the speed of the wind increases. Due to this, the wind blows in a parallel direction to the isobars.

FUN FACT

According to a theory on geostrophic winds, if you stand facing the Southern Hemisphere, the low-pressure winds will always be to your left. If you stand facing the Northern Hemisphere, the low-pressure winds will always be to your right.

PATTERNS AND ZONES OF WIND

The global climate is affected by wind patterns. Wind patterns tell us in which direction the wind moves and what it contains. Heat from the Sun gives wind the energy to move. As the wind moves, it makes warm and cool spots around Earth in an uneven manner.

Sea and land breeze

Inland areas tend to warm up under the Sun's heat during the day. The air also warms and rises higher up into the atmosphere. The cool air from the nearby oceans takes the place of this air and form winds. As the evening approaches, the inland starts experiencing cool breeze. At night, the temperature in the inland areas cools down and the air begins to drop lower. This area receives land breeze. The air above the ocean now warms up instead.

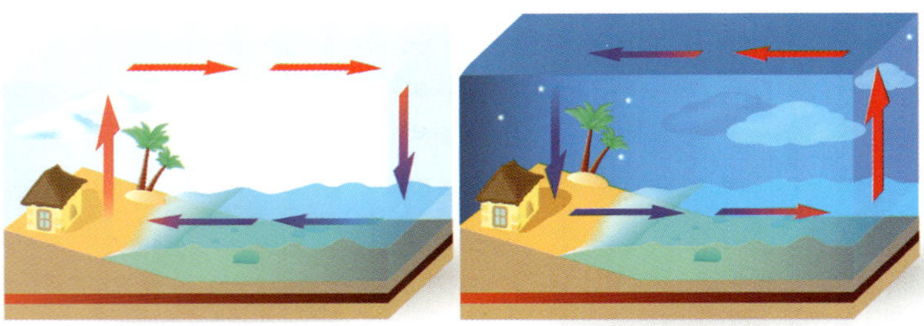

Diagram depicting the movement of air.

Global wind patterns

Even though cold and warm air move, the poles always remain cold and the equator always remains hot. This is because of global wind patterns which permanently affect the climate of a place.

The Coriolis effect

The Coriolis effect, which is caused by Earth's rotation on its tilted axis, pulls air from the north and south directions. When warm air rises upwards, it spreads to north and south. As it cools, it begins to sink lower. The Coriolis effect forces a curve upon the moving air. This causes the wind from the northeast, which are coming from the Northern Hemisphere, converge with the winds from the southeast, which are coming from the Southern Hemisphere. They are called "trade winds". They move across the tropical zones.

Westerlies and Easterlies

As we move from the equator, the wind blowing over the surface tends to move in a direction towards the Polar Regions. Due to the Coriolis effect, the winds are forced to turn to the opposite direction, or towards the west. These winds are called the "westerlies".

On the other hand, the 60°N and 60°S latitudes have cool winds that move towards the equator. They are also forced to bend and move in the opposite direction, or towards the east. They are called the "easterlies".

Horse latitudes

A horse latitude is a weather zone. The 30–35°N and 30–35°S latitudes have horse latitudes. They lie between the westerlies and the easterlies. This zone has a dry and warm climate. All horse latitudes have prevailing winds. However, they are light. These winds are only strong for some time. The Kalahari Desert of South America is a part of the horse latitude zone.

Winds sweep over the Kalahari dunes in South Africa.

Doldrums

An intertropical convergence zone is the formation that takes place in an area where trade winds from two directions converge. The prevailing winds that are surrounding this area tend to be very weak. Due to this factor, the weather remains relatively calm throughout the year. This surrounding area is called "doldrums".

The intertropical convergence zone overlaps the equator. When the Sun's heat warms up the equatorial region, the hot air rises upwards. The hot air travels north and south. This leads to the creation of horse latitudes. When this air cools down, the doldrums return to the equator in the form of trade winds. Some doldrums may even lead to the formation of westerlies.

Sailors were horrified by doldrums

In the past, maritime soldiers and sailors often shuddered at the mention of a doldrum. This is because their ships would become stuck there.

FUN FACT

As the wind reaches the middle of a low-pressure zone, it begins to migrate upwards. This might result in a storm. On the other hand, in a high-pressure zone, the air at the centre tends to sink from above. This can produce a calm, gentle weather.

Satellite photo of a storm.

Highs and lows

The mid-latitude regions of Earth are the hub for high-pressure and low-pressure zones. As we know, air moves from the high-pressure zones to the low-pressure zones. High-pressure zones are called "highs". Low-pressure zones are called "lows".

The wind, while moving from one zone to the other, coils under the Coriolis effect. We experience high and low temperature as the highs and lows move because of the prevailing winds.

Formation of Clouds

Have you ever watched the clouds in the sky? You will notice that all clouds have different shapes. Sometimes, the sky has a few clouds and sometimes it has many. On sunny days, clouds appear to be white. On rainy days, they appear grey. The clouds in the sky are formed from little drops of water or small crystals of ice.

Cloud condensation nuclei

Cloud condensation nuclei are particles of dust that are found in the atmosphere. These dust particles are first formed in the air closer to Earth's surface. They are formed from pollutants such as vehicle smoke, gases from industries and other such things that cause air pollution.

Water vapour forms droplets of water when it attaches itself onto these condensation nuclei. Ice crystals and water vapour are also formed on the basis of altitude and how humid the air is.

Pollution leads to the formation of cloud condensation nuclei.

Dew point

The moist or humid air begins to expand once it travels higher into the atmosphere. As it expands, it cools and reaches its "dew point". This dew point is nothing but the formation of water droplets which are then open to the sky and the surrounding atmosphere. Air can only reach its dew point at a time when the weather is calm and when there is a light breeze. If the surrounding temperature reaches freezing point, ice crystals are formed instead of water droplets.

FUN FACT

Just like trees provide shade to Earth, clouds provide shade too. This prevents sunlight from directly hitting plants. Without clouds, we would all be feeling much warmer!

How are ice crystals formed in the atmosphere?

We cannot see the tiny ice crystals or drops of water in the sky as they are too far away from us. The air in the atmosphere contains some moisture. This makes the air humid. When the humid air becomes cooler, the water vapour in the air compresses to form crystals of ice or droplets of water.

Saturation point

As water droplets or ice crystals form in the air, there might come a time when the air becomes saturated with it. "Saturated" means that the air cannot hold more water vapour or ice crystals. Warmer air holds more water vapour than cooler air. So, as the air becomes cooler, the water vapour is sort of squeezed out of the air like a sponge. This is when clouds form. The tiny water droplets or ice crystals that form are then packed together tightly.

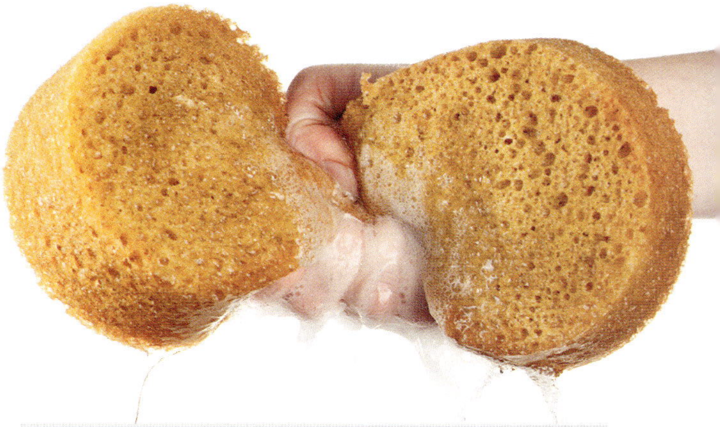

Why are clouds white?

The tightly packed crystals or droplets give clouds their white colour. As a result, the sunlight that hits the clouds is reflected back. So, when we look at the clouds, we see a white colour.

On the other hand, clouds darken as they fill up with water vapour and form raindrops. The space between the crystals or water drops increases so that the sunlight is not reflected as much. So when we look up we see grey or black clouds.

Classification of clouds

Clouds are classified on the basis of their altitude or height from Earth's surface:

- **Cirrus clouds:**
  The highest clouds in the atmosphere are called "cirrus clouds". They can rise to nearly 20,000 feet from Earth's surface. These clouds do not produce any form of precipitation as they are extremely thin. But because of this the surrounding area has calm weather. As the temperature at this altitude is very low, these clouds are entirely formed of ice crystals.
- **Altostratus clouds:**
  These are flat clouds. They are called "altocumulus" if they become puffy. They are at a distance of 6000-7000 feet from Earth's surface. They produce precipitation such as rain or snow, but this does not reach the surface.
- **Stratus clouds:**
  The clouds we see on Earth are called "stratus clouds". They lie immediately below the altostratus clouds.

WATER FROM THE SKY

A cloud is like a tap and precipitation is like the water flowing from it. There are different forms of precipitation at different places. Some places might see it as snow and some might see it as rain. But precipitation can also be in the form of hail or sleet.

Importance of precipitation

The common thing between the four types of precipitation is that it is all water that falls from the clouds in the sky but in different forms. The precipitation of an area greatly affects its vegetation. The types of plants that grow, what they grow and how they grow are all affected by precipitation. It even affects human life. While one type of precipitation might be beneficial to human life, another type might be very dangerous to it.

Formation of precipitation

Water vapour slowly forms water droplets or ice crystals, which then form clouds. Sometimes, they form fog. The water vapour collects dust and condenses to form cloud condensation nuclei. Precipitation forms along the cloud condensation nuclei. Once clouds reach their saturation point, precipitation changes to form either a liquid like rain or a solid like snow.

Rain is a type of precipitation.

Drizzle and shower

Rain is seen as a drizzle or shower. Light rain with few drops of water is called, "drizzle". Anything heavier than a drizzle is called a "shower". It usually lasts for a shorter time than a drizzle but has more range.

Precipitation and water cycle

The water cycle would not exist without precipitation. Precipitation allows water from the atmosphere to fall to Earth's surface as snow or rain. With the Sun's heat, this water evaporates as water vapour and returns to the atmosphere. The water vapour then forms clouds, which again form precipitation. If there was no precipitation, Earth would not receive fresh water. Without fresh water, human life would be in great danger.

Diagram of the water cycle.

Low rainfall, snowfall and melting glaciers are indicators of global warming.

Sleet

Around cooler areas, raindrops freeze on their way to the surface. These drops become thicker and have a more solid form. This is called "sleet" or "ice pellets". Sleet is wetter and mushier than rain.

Rain

Raindrops form in the atmosphere around cloud condensation nuclei. Over time, these raindrops grow in size. Slowly, they become too big and saturate the cloud. As the cloud cannot hold them anymore, they begin to fall towards the surface. On the way, they merge with other drops to grow in size. Rainfall is the most commonly seen precipitation on Earth. This is because more parts of Earth receive rain. Snow, hail and sleet are seen in fewer parts.

Virga

Precipitation does not always reach Earth's surface. Sometimes, precipitation falls from the cloud. But as it falls, it comes into contact with warmer temperature and evaporates. This water vapour joins the water cycle directly in this stage and rises up again to form clouds.

Hail and snow

Hailstones and snow look different because snow has a complex structure. On the other hand, hailstones are just water droplets that have frozen. They are like crystals of ice, somewhat similar to ice cubes. Hailstones are hard while snow is soft. Hailstones can be harmful. Snowfall is peaceful and calm.

Hailstones are called "frozenwater droplets".

FUN FACT

Raindrops are commonly drawn as little droplets of tears. However, real raindrops actually have a spherical or round shape.

Hail

Storm clouds are called "cumulus". These clouds rise to great altitudes and begin to grow in size. When they come into contact with hot air, they begin to produce thunderstorms. Cumulus clouds that produce thunderstorms are called "cumulonimbus".

The water droplets in these clouds that come into contact with dust almost immediately freeze into solids. These solids are blown upwards into the clouds as "hailstones". As they go upwards, they combine with other solid water droplets. These hailstones fall on Earth as "hail". Hailstones are like little rocks, but they crumble when they come into contact with the surface.

Hailstorm in Sweden.

FOG AND FROST

In very cold places, the water vapour or moisture in the atmosphere solidifies once it touches the ground or any surface near the ground. It can also form on open objects such as plants, trees, cars and windows. The moisture crystallises and appears white to our eyes. This is called "frost".

Dew point and frost

The dew point is a point at which air becomes cold and then turns into a liquid. This liquid then becomes solid. Frost appears on any surface that passes its dew point.

Fog

"Fog" is a name given to clouds that float very close to the surface and even touch the surface.
Fog is formed when water vapour condenses to make small water droplets close to the surface. These water droplets combine together so that we can see them. A fog can be thick or thin. We cannot see past a thick fog. Places that experience heavy fog also experience heavy frost.

Morning frost seen on the blades of the grass.

How does fog form?

Fog takes place in extremely humid climate. Fog can only form when there is lots of water vapour present in the air. Just as clouds cannot form without dust or cloud condensation nuclei, fog cannot form without dust or particles of dirt. Fog forms in places that experience air pollution.

The water vapour in the air condenses around the particles of air pollution and forms the clouds of fog. Fog can even form when salt is present in the surroundings. Sea fog forms over salty bodies of water when they come in contact with the surface.

Radiation frost

Frost cannot form when there are lots of clouds in the air. This is because clouds blanket Earth. They hold the heat or radiation rising upwards from the ground. Because there are clouds, there will be some wind. The wind mixes whatever air is trapped in the clouds and spreads it around to create an even temperature.

On the other hand, if there are no clouds, the radiation and heat from the ground rise upwards and escape into the atmosphere. Now, cooler air is present near the ground while warmer air is rising in the atmosphere. This loss of heat causes the surface to freeze and form a frost.

Advection frost

When a big cold air mass or a cold front moves along a certain region, it leads to the formation of an advection frost. At the time of an advection frost, the winds become gusty. The cloud cover can either be very thick or there might not be any clouds in the sky. Starting from the clouds, cold air might rise 2 km into the air.

Advection frost forms in the shape of tiny spikes of ice. An advection frost can be moderate or severe.

Advection frost looks like tiny spikes of ice.

Hoar frost

When the temperature drops below 0 °C, it leads to the formation of frost. If the temperature is above 0 °C, it leads to the formation of dew.

As a result of the low temperature, the air cools beyond the saturation point. When this happens, the water vapour condenses and directly leads to the formation of ice crystals. These ice crystals are formed on the surfaces of open objects.

Frost on trees.

Frost gathering on windows.

Window frost

Window frost, as the name suggests, forms on the windows of houses and vehicles. This type of frost is formed when one side of the window receives cool air and the other side receives warm air. It occurs mainly in cold places that experience some snow as precipitation. Thick, double-paned windows do not experience this type of frost.

FUN FACT

We cannot see through thick fog. Sometimes, the fog rises so high and has such a high range that even large monuments cannot be visible from afar. The Golden Gate Bridge in San Francisco and the London Bridge in England are sometimes completely hidden by fog.

Rime

Rime forms in cold places with wet climate. This type of frost appears very quickly on the surface. Rime can even form if there is no snow in the air. Cold winds can form rime. When lots of rime collects on a surface, it gives the appearance of solid ice.

Frost on a leaf

TROPICAL CLIMATE

Climate is influenced by the location, topography, elevation and latitude of a place. The continent in which a place is located is also an important factor that affects its climate. It is divided into different types. These types then have their own sub climates.

Tropical climate

The major types of climates are tropical climates, dry climates, mild climates, continental climates and polar climates. The tropical zone experiences the tropical climate. It is divided into three main types. These are the tropical wet climate, the tropical monsoon climate and the tropical wet and dry climate.

- **Tropical wet climate:** Rainforests experience the tropical wet climate. Rainforests have the easiest climate to predict. They have regular annual rainfall as well as a warm, humid climate. The temperature undergoes constant changes. The lowest day temperatures ranges from 20-23°C. The highest day temperature ranges from 30-32°C. The places lying 10° to the north and south of the equator have tropical wet climate.
- **Tropical monsoon climate:** West Africa and South Asia experience the tropical monsoon climate. India has a tropical monsoon climate. "Monsoon" is the name for a wind system. This wind system travels down a path for six months, then takes the reverse path for the remaining six months of the year. During the summer, these wind systems move towards the land from the sea. During the winter, they move from the land towards the sea. As a result, in these climates, maximum rainfall is experienced during the summers.
- **Tropical wet and dry climate:** This type of climate experiences all three seasons. It lies close to the equator. During the summer, the weather is cold and dry. During the winter, the weather is warm and dry. The third season is hot and moist. During the third season, the climate resembles the tropical wet climate. Kolkata in India has a tropical wet and dry climate.

Rainforests have a tropical wet climate.

Deciduous forest.

DRY CLIMATE

Dry climate is experienced in those parts of the world that have low precipitation. These places are mostly found in higher latitudes. Dry climate is further divided into arid and semi-arid climate.

Arid and semi-arid climate

Tall mountains block warm and humid wind masses from entering these climates. The annual rainfall in these places is low. A place that has arid climate receives less than 30 cm of annual rainfall. Semi-arid climates have 25 to 50 cm of annual rainfall. Arid and semi-arid climates experience daily variations in temperature. They also experience the hottest climates. On the other hand, semi-arid sub climate zones have prairies and savannahs as they receive a good amount of rainfall.

Deserts have arid or semi-arid climates.

Mild climate

Mild climates are found in temperate zones. The main cause for this type of climate is the latitude or location within a continent. Places that experience a mild climate have short, warm summers and mild winters. The weather is cool during the winters and a lot of the annual rainfall occurs at this time.

Mediterranean climate and marine west coast climate

The mild climate type has a sub climate called the "Mediterranean climate". This is because most of the places that experience this climate lie along the Mediterranean Sea. These places have clear skies, very little rainfall and cold nights. The marine west coast climate has cool, long winters with very little rainfall.

Extremes of dry climate

Death Valley, California holds the world record for the hottest recorded weather. On 10th July, 1913, the temperature was recorded as 56.7 °C. The Atacama Desert is the driest place on Earth and lies in the dry and arid climate zone. A place called Arica which lies in South America has an annual rainfall of less than 0.05 cm.

Humid subtropical climate

This is another sub climate type of the mild climate. Places like Sydney, Shanghai and Georgia experience this type of climate. These places have extremely cold winters. They receive an annual precipitation of 75–160 cm.

CONTINENTAL AND POLAR CLIMATE

Places that have continental climate are actually transition zones. They lie between mild climates and polar climates. As a result, these places experience sudden and powerful changes in the weather.

Warm summer climate

The continental climate is further divided into three types—warm summer, cool summer and subarctic. As the name suggests, places with a warm summer climate have warm summers. Their climate is similar to the tropical monsoon climate but far less intense. It is different than the other climate types as the weather tends to be more moist and humid. As a result, this climate type is also called "humid continental climate". It is experienced in the Eastern European countries.

European regions have humid climates.

Subarctic climate

Subarctic climates are known for their long winters and short summers. There is little precipitation experienced here. Whatever precipitation reaches the surface falls in the form of snow. The air has little humidity. Most of Alaska experiences this climate type. Siberia is another place that has the subarctic climate.

Subarctic climates have long, cold winters.

Cool summer climate

Places that have the cool summer climate experience low temperatures. The precipitation in these places falls in the form of snow. There are cool air masses continuously blowing from the Arctic regions. During the winter, the weather gets harsh and bitter. The places that experience cool summer climates lie close to the subarctic climates. Parts of Russia experience the cool summer climate.

Arctic regions have cool climates.

Polar climate

The Arctic Circle and Antarctic Circle experience the polar climate. This climate type experiences extremely short summers, and long and intense winters. The polar climate is further categorised into the tundra climate and the ice cap.

Tundra climate

Places with the tundra climate type have many plants and animals. The temperatures here can rise to 10 °C during the summers. Beautiful wildflowers are spread out over the tundra regions. The vegetation attracts different types of birds. During the winter, these birds tend to migrate to warmer climates. In the summer, they feed on fish and insects in the area.

Whales are the most notable wildlife of the tundra region. They feed on the nutritious microscopic organisms present in the water. Unlike the ice cap climates, the tundra region enjoys a thriving population which has adapted itself to live in the cold climate.

The terrestrial and aquatic life varies as per the climate.

Climate change

Unlike weather, climate takes a very long time to change. Climatic change is a slow process which takes hundreds of years to realise. Earth tilting on its axis, tectonic plate movement and sudden volcanic eruptions can all lead to climatic changes.

Ice cap climates

The ice cap climate type is home to very few living organisms. This is because of its freezing climate. This climate type experiences short summers, however the temperatures remain freezing during the season. The ice cap climate type is called so because ice covers the land all throughout the year.

There is very little precipitation experienced in the ice cap climate, as a result of which this area has clear skies almost throughout the year. Antarctica is the most notable area that has the ice cap climate. It is a polar desert.

Example of a polar desert.

FUN FACT

It is believed that the Sahara Desert was once covered by an ocean. This was a very long time ago. Changes in the climate in and around this region brought about the formation of one of the driest deserts in the world.

Global warming

Human beings have been cutting down forests for years. The forest cover of the world has reduced drastically. Also, fossil fuels are being used up at alarming rates. Both of these activities have led to greenhouse gases (methane, water vapour, ozone and carbon dioxide) to be released into the atmosphere.

These gases absorb the heat from the Sun and warm up the surrounding atmosphere, which in turn warms up the climate experienced around the world. As a result, the world has been getting warmer. This is called "global warming".

Human activities have drastically affected the polar climate.

GLOBAL WARMING

The term "global warming" describes a climatic change. It is the ongoing climatic change taking place on Earth. Global warming refers to the rising temperatures of the ocean and air.

Changing times

In the past, Earth has experienced much higher and much lower temperatures. But global warming is considered an important instance of climatic change as it is taking place now and is taking place at an alarming rate.

Cause of global warming

Global warming is a result of the natural cycle of change in temperatures (as seen in the causes behind the ice ages). However, if it were the only cause, climatic change would have taken place at a much slower rate. Due to human activities, the climate has been getting warmer at great speed. This change in climate can affect various species of life. It is a fear among global scientists that not many people can adapt to the increasing temperatures.

Global warming is said to be a serious threat to life on Earth.

The greenhouse effect

"The greenhouse effect" is the name given to the role of human beings in the speeding up of global warming. It also describes the effect of greenhouse gases such as nitrogen oxide, methane, carbon dioxide, fluorinated gases and chlorofluorocarbons (CFCs) on the atmosphere. They are naturally present in the atmosphere. They are like insulators which block the heat that is reflecting back from Earth's surface. Without greenhouse gases, Earth's temperatures would be much cooler, thus freezing the planet and making it impossible for many organisms to survive.

Recent changes in temperatures

In the recent years, Earth's surface temperatures have risen to an average of about 0.74 °C. This change has taken place within the past century. The surface temperatures of the land are increasing at a faster rate than that of the ocean. This change in temperature is also more prominent in the northern latitudes where ice caps have been melting.

Role of human beings

Since the industrial era in the 1700s, until today, various human activities have increased the amount of greenhouse gases that are present in the atmosphere. The presence of carbon dioxide in the atmosphere within the past three decades has increased by 80 per cent. The insulating effect of the greenhouse gases has increased which is the major cause behind global warming.

The greenhouse effect.

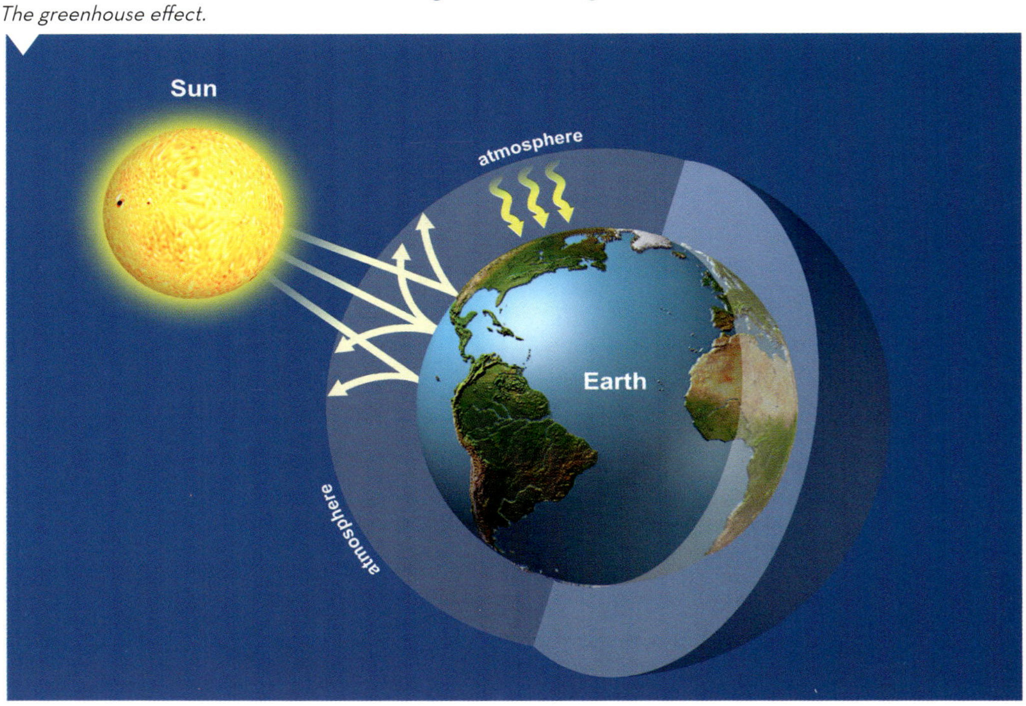